D0120742

"BONNIE MONTROSE."

POEMS AND SONGS,

BY

WM . F. M'HARDY,

" A MEARNS LADDIE "

"Some rhyme a neebor's name to lash;
Some rhyme (vain thought!) for needfu' cash;
Some rhyme to court the countra clash,
    An' raise a din;
For me, an aim I never fash –
    I rhyme for fun!"

- BURNS.

MONTROSE:
GEORGE A. BOWMAN, 48 HIGH STREET,
PRINTER AND PUBLISHER.
1899.

Mereo Books

1A The Wool Market Dyer Street Cirencester Gloucestershire GL7 2PR
An imprint of Memoirs Publishing www.mereobooks.com

Bonnie Montrose: 978-1-86151-361-8

First published in Great Britain in 2014
by Mereo Books, an imprint of Memoirs Publishing

Copyright ©2014

Wm. F. M.'HARDY has asserted his right under the Copyright Designs and Patents
Act 1988 to be identified as the author of this work.

This book is a work of fiction and except in the case of historical fact any resemblance to actual
persons living or dead is purely coincidental.

A CIP catalogue record for this book is available from the British Library.

This book is sold subject to the condition that it shall not by way of trade or otherwise be lent,
resold, hired out or otherwise circulated without the publisher's prior consent in any form of
binding or cover, other than that in which it is published and without a similar condition,
including this condition being imposed on the subsequent purchaser.

The address for Memoirs Publishing Group Limited can be found at
www.memoirspublishing.com

The Memoirs Publishing Group Ltd Reg. No. 7834348

The Memoirs Publishing Group supports both The Forest Stewardship Council® (FSC®) and
the PEFC® leading international forest-certification organisations. Our books carrying both the
FSC label and the PEFC® and are printed on FSC®-certified paper. FSC® is the only
forest-certification scheme supported by the leading environmental organisations including
Greenpeace. Our paper procurement policy can be found at
www.memoirspublishing.com/environment

Typeset by Wiltshire Associates Publisher Services Ltd. Printed and bound in Great Britain by
Printondemand-Worldwide, Peterborough PE2 6XD

CONTENTS.

———◆———

CONTENTS – Continued

Foreword

———◆◆———

This book has been republished after an interval of 115 years in memory of the author, my great-grandfather, William F McHardy, who I never had the chance to know. A special thank you to my grandfather and Dad, also William McHardy, for giving me a wonderful childhood and my second home of Montrose. Also my Great Uncle James and family, who we have lost touch with over the years.

I miss but have fond memories of my wonderful Gran Agnes, my Mum, Margaret, and the generations that have since passed. I promised you all the original book would be passed on and it now belongs to my son William's first son, Will.

I never thought for one second the book could be brought back from near extinction, but it has and now a new audience can read the poems, songs and thoughts from over a hundred years past.

Thank you to everyone for buying it, and I hope you enjoy the journey back in time to an Old Montrose as he knew, its places and its people.

I still have a love for this beautiful town and all the 'Gable Enders' past and present. Places preserved in time like Frosts the Baker, The Black Horse, The Lochside Bar, Montrose Links, Melville Gardens, Limes Guesthouse, Montrose Basin, Ferryden, North Esk Road, The Grove, Bridge of Dun, House of Dun, Seafront Splash or Sleepy Hillock, the list itself endless.

Time goes by so quickly, so if you get any chance, like a new generation of our family, come visit and enjoy our Bonnie Montrose.

A special thank you to Cancer Research UK and The British Heart Foundation on my 70th birthday this year, with 40% of any profit made being split evenly between these charities. With a further 50p of any profit from each book going to Tesco's Charity of the Year, as a thank you to everyone for their support.

Kindest Regards
Robert T McHardy snr

Thank you from Bob McHardy

———•◦•———

Thank you firstly for all the support in getting this book back to print and to everyone for buying it, I really want everyone to enjoy the journey back through Bonnie Montrose and hope one day you take the chance to go and see this beautiful coastal town.

I would like to take this opportunity to thank the following people for working with me on this project:

Chris Newton, Tony Tingle, Ray Lipscombe and their team at Memoirs Publishing. www.memoirsbooks.co.uk

Elly Donovan and her team at Elly Donovan PR. www.ellydonovan.co.uk

Harry Fraser and his team at Fraser Web Design. www.fraserwebdesign.co.uk

Brian Traynor and his team at Traynor Accounting. www.traynoraccounting.co.uk

Andrew Cockburn his the team at Oswalds. www.oswalds.co.uk

Carol Cassells and her team at TSB Bank Cumbernauld and Business Banking. www.tsb.co.uk

Margaret Ann Smart, Jemma Vallance and the team at Let's Party Scotland. www.letspartyscotland.co.uk

Simon Gillespie and his team at The British Heart Foundation www.bhf.org.uk

Dr Harper S Kumal and his team at Cancer Research UK
http://www.cancerresearchuk.org/

Dave Lewis, Alison Horner, and Paula Wales
and everyone at Tesco PLC
www.tesco.com

A special mention to Forbes Inglis a local freelance Writer and
Photographer and columnist for the Montrose Review and Mr A Hogg,
of Henry Hogg, local Newsagent and Book Cellar in in Montrose,
Marlene and Graeme Scott at The Limes Guest House and everyone
in the town for all your assistance.

Marlene and Graeme Scott at the Limes Guest House.

A special thanks to William McHardy, David, Ellie and Sienna
Blackwood, Colin Offord and Neil Boyd for all your input with the
website, Frank O'Donnell, Frank Hollywood and David 'Red' Lillie.
Thank you for your friendship.

Frank O'Donnell, Frank Hollywood, David 'Red'Lillie.

And lastly to all my Friends and Family for all your love and support.

"Happy 70th Birthday Dad".

"Hi Mummy and Papa, I am home".

All my love

Bob
www.bonniemontrose.co.uk

v

A Special Word

To the William McHardys I never knew, not forgetting my grandfather, who left me the original book from our past generations. Thank you to my brother, who has managed to bring the book back for everyone to enjoy once more.

Will McHardy

My son William will carry the name forward and through his family, God willing, in years to come.

I tried to explain the William McHardy history to my son, and he simply said, "Daddy, I am the real Will McHardy".

I always love to come and visit Montrose, with St Cyrus being the place I have come to love the most. The beautiful people, places and sounds written about in the book, have aged and grown over the annals of time.

Perhaps we have all moved on over the years, but to visit Montrose is something everyone can come, experience and enjoy.

See you all soon

William F McHardy, Maureen, Declan, Kieran, Aimee, and Will xxxxxx

Thank you from
Robert McHardy Senior

———◆———

I must thank and give special recognition to Dr Pettigrew and everyone at Springburn Health Centre, the late Dr Hogg and Mr Crooks and everyone at Stobhill Hospital.

Not forgetting Dr Twaddle and Partners at Abronhill Health Centre, Mr Barr, Dr McAlpine, Dr Murphy and everyone at Monkland's Hospital.

Lastly to Cancer Research UK and the British Heart Foundation, whose pioneering work has ultimately given me 20 years of life (come January 2015) and I will always be grateful and hope the book raises funds to help you continue your life saving work. As well as generating funds each year for Tesco's chosen charity of the year.

Sincerely

Robert T McHardy snr

Dedication

In loving memory of a wonderful, inspirational woman,
and my other mum, Mrs Catherine Kirkland, who passed
away in March this year.

Catherine Kirkland
1919-2014

All our love
Robert snr and all the family

Bonnie Montrose.

PREFACE.

---·:·---

DEAR READER,

I feel a sort of a peculiar feeling lurking in my veins in regard to the publication of this my first book of poems, as to how they will be received by the public. It is with grateful heart that I thank the many subscribers who have so honourably come forward to assist me. Critics there will be, no doubt; they will find errors in plenty, but don't judge your humble servant too harshly, for we are like receding waves rolling over the sands of time, to be swallowed up sooner or later in the unforeseen hereafter, where critics, foes, and friends, meet face to face.

Standing by the sea shore, one cannot but listen to the murmur of the waters of the great ocean as the waves lap, lap upon the sandy shore, then the whish of the receding waves as they recoil back into the vortex of the never-ceasing music of the mighty ocean. So is the mind of the bard never at rest; sometimes soaring away in the sunny skies, by the lovely dale, on the ocean wave, at the fireside at e'en, and in the land of dreams, inhaling that blissful lesson which, alas, so many are ignorant of viz: the cultivation of the finer feelings.

If my little book, "Bonnie Montrose," find a corner in your bookshelf, it is my only wish that when you turn over the leaves and read, it may bring to your memory happy thoughts of long ago.

Your humble friend,

WM. F. M. 'HARDY.

INTRODUCTION.

———◆———

"Montrose: my ain auld happy hame,
There's music in thy couthy name;
Remembrance like a mornin' dream
Flees aye to thee;
To our loved haunts by wood or stream,
Or dashing sea."

— SMART'S "RAMBLING RHYMES."

ONTROSE, a Royal Burgh and seaport, gives
the title of Duke to the Chief of the noble
family of Graham. The town is situated on a flat
sandy peninsula formed by the German Ocean, the
river South Esk, and a large expanse of water called
the Basin. It is accounted one of the first provincial
towns in Scotland. The seal of the town is
countenanced by an ornament of roses, and bears the
following motto: "Mare ditat, rosa decorat" – the sea
enriches and the rose adorns. Its name is connected
with many important events in Scottish history. It is
mentioned by Froissart as the port from which Sir
James Douglas embarked in 1330, with a numerous
and splendid retinue, on a pilgrimage to the Holy
Land, carrying along with him the heart of Robert

INTRODUCTION – continued

———◆———

Bruce. It is distinguished as the first place in Scotland where the Greek language was taught, by teachers brought over by John Erskine of Dun, in 1534; and as having sent forth from its seminary the celebrated scholar, Andrew Melville. It was the birthplace of the warlike Marquis of Montrose, and the house in which he was born was occupied as an inn a good many years ago. It was the first port made by the French fleet in December, 1715, with the Chevalier on board; and that Prince embarked at the same place in February of the following year.

Standing on the high ground on Rossie Braes, on the south side of the town, looking north when it is high water, the Basin on the left is like a mirrored lake, with the finely cultivated and fertile fields rising gracefully from its shores. The numerous surrounding mansions occupied by the nobility of the county, basking in the shelter of thick and clustering woods, and away to the east the romantic cliffs of St. Cyrus bursts on our view, with the towering Grampians in the background, presents one of the grandest scenes in nature in the United Kingdom.

INTRODUCTION – continued

————◆————

The Links are situated between the town and the sea, and are amongst the most extensive of any in Scotland; finely formed by nature for the favourite game of golf, which is greatly practiced.

There is a well-equipped bathing station, attended by a qualified rescue. The bathing coaches are largely taken advantage of during the season, great numbers of visitors frequenting the town in summer. The golf course, the bathing station, expansive Links, and sea shore, are great attractions. There is a comfortable Pavilion with a verandah at the bathing station, where visitors can have shelter and refreshments.

The public gardens are worthy of attention. The Melville and Panmure Gardens are very neat and beautifully laid out, they are exceedingly pretty when the flowers and trees are in foliage, and are admired by all who have the pleasure of seeing them in the summer and autumn months. There are numerous comfortable seats planted here and there throughout the gardens and Links, where you can rest and have a look around, while you inhale the aroma of the sweet smelling flowers. In the Melville Gardens there is a well-kept bowling green, where an hour can be spent pleasantly for a small charge.

Entering from Bridge Street you reach the West End Park, a nice stretch of grass, with a well-kept winding path running through the centre of it, terminating at the green of the Montrose Bowling Club. There are some nice plots of flowers in the park, and the walls running along the east side of it, which were at one time washed by the waters of the Basin, are covered with ivy, which make the place rather charming.

The town is greatly indebted to the late Provost Scott, for the designs of the Melville and Panmure Gardens, the West End Park, and other improvements. He was a man of taste, and his works will make his name a household word in the town for generations.

POEMS AND SONGS.

BONNIE MONTROSE

ON a sunny shore by the ocean wave,
Where the cool eastern breeze the riplets lave,
And the lovely sands reach far, far along,
In the sun's rays dance to the ocean song,
By the grassy Links like a carpet spread -
The home of the golfer, the daisy's bed –
There it stands, loved by all who comes and goes,
The Eden of Scotland – Bonnie Montrose.

In the West End Park, on a summer's day,
Where the sweet-scented flowers bloom fresh and gay,
And ivy clings to the old sea wall,
Like a phantom scene in a fairy's hall.
At the twilight eve, in the golden west,
When the sunbeams gleam on the mountain crest,
No lovlier picture art could disclose
Than the sun's good-night to bonnie Montrose.

The home of our childhood and schoolboy days,
With glee all joined in their innocent plays;
A game at the bools, a kick at the ba',
Ye'd wonder hoo cheery the time slipp'd awa'.
Some camsteerie loons wad kick up a shine,
Aff wi' their jackets, and stand up in line,
Spit in their hands, cry, "I'm ready, here goes" –
There's grit in the youth of bonnie Montrose.

Some leave the auld toon for lands far awa',
Like true-hearted Scotchmen to stand or to fa',
Born sons of freedom, and true to the core,
Brave on the ocean, and loved on the shore:
Yet though they may dwell under sunny skies,
Their land of adoption highly may prize,
When laid down to rest for a calm repose,
They dream happy dreams of bonnie Montrose.

The strangers in summer seek our sand-girt shore
To sniff the sea breeze their health to restore,
And bathe in the tide of the ocean blue,
To colour their pale cheeks with a rosy hue.
The golf course is free, and second to none,
And all are made welcome to play thereon;
Freedom is sweet as the scent of the rose,
Strangers enjoy it in bonnie Montrose.

Away for a sail on the silv'ry tide,
With a trusty steersman our boat to guide,
Down the fleeting Esk she skims away
Across the Bar to the open bay;
Now she glides along with a steady breeze,
Like a stately gull as he breasts the seas;
"For port," says the skipper, "the tide now flows,"
So we're safe once more in bonnie Montrose.

'Tis our home, we'll love it for evermore,
For memory's sake its name we adore;
May its sons and daughters lead noble lives –
The sons good husbands, the daughters good wives;
May the star of peace shine around its shores,
And the full hand of plenty fill its stores,
And the strong arm of love around all close
At their last farewell to bonnie Montrose.

LIVING TRUTHS

MAN is subject to many trials
      Of different kinds, hard and severe;
And stumbling blocks fall in our way,
      Which fill our very hearts with fear.

To silly ways we're prone to yield,
      And selfish fancies fill our mind;
Our very thoughts are ofttimes weak –
      Perfection's brink we cannot find.

Ofttimes we fain would brag and boast
      What we can do, and what we've done;
With haughty pride we ofttimes sneer
      At others' faults – blind to our own.

Poor, mortal man, aye discontent,
      And will be here for evermore;
To satisfy us no one could,
      Though richest treasures filled our store.

We envy oft our brother's lot,
      And curse his luck within our breast;
With joy would dance upon his grave,
      If we were in his riches drest.

To-day our merry laugh resounds,
> Both mirth and fun we glory in;
To-morrow finds us dull and sad,
> Which shows there's something wrong within.

To-day we build up mountains high,
> To-morrow we intend to climb;
Alas! to-morrow ne'er we'll see,
> The bugle sounds " 'this time, 'this time."

To criticise man's sojourn here,
> Or purge the deeds which he has done,
And pass the Judge without a flaw,
> Ah! Truth replies, "there is not one."

Life is but a passing shadow,
> And veiled in mist just like a dream,
Floating on and on for ever,
> Down the vale like a running stream.

Till swallowed up in kindred soil,
> Our bodies mixed with mother earth,
There to lie till the trumpet sound
> That great event – our second birth.

THE WASHIN' DAY

(Dedicated to my respected friend "A.S.")

THE washin' day, the washin' day,
O leese me on the washin' day;
Mark weel your steps, for rough's the way,
That day o' days – the washin' day.

O little does young callants ken
The drees they dree when marriet men,
The brunt they stan' at their fire en',
Especially on the washin' day.

The ither morn, afore daylicht,
I waukened in an awfu' fright,
The wife roarin' wi' a' her micht –
"Getup, gudeman, its washin' day."

I hirsled oot below the claes,
And in my breeks I stapp'd my taes;
I claws my pow and little says,
The morning' o' the washin' day.

The floor clad ower wi' dirty duds;
The wife up tae the oxters thuds
Amang the froth and soapy suds,
Scrub, scrubbin' on the washin' day.

Ocht can she dae but girn an' flyte,
While I, poor man, dejected-like,
Maun wash the bairns an' feed the tyke,
I'm or'ley on the washin' day.

I've tea tae mask an' fish tae fry,
Assist the wife I then maun try,
In hangin' oot the claes tae dry,
Ilk mornin' on the washin' day.

I hurries aff then tae my wark;
The passin' curs at me they bark;
They think I'm bent-set for a lark –
They little ken it's washin' day.

For dinner cauld kail, sometimes sour,
For which I aye maun crouch and cour,
In fact, aft, aft I've aught but stoor
For dinner on washin' day.

It's nicht at last, the claes a' dry,
A' fau'ded up, an' laid safe bye;
Richt glad it's ower, in troth, am I –
O gloomy, gruesome washin' day.

My faithfu' cronie, watch your eye;
If e're you join the nuptial tie,
Aye "jouk an' lat the jaw gae by"
Upon that day – the washin' day.

.

Aboot it I need say nae mair,
But wish that day may aye keep fair,
For, if it rains, I do declare
You'll sing – "Farewell, O washin' day."

Dear friend, success to you through life,
A happy hame, a lovin' wife;
An' may the bonnie bairns by rife;
They mak' a cheerfu' washin' day.

May went ne'er enter at your door;
Aye lots o' claes, an' meat galore;
Your aumry fu' an' rinnin' o'er,
An' aye a drouthy washin' day.

LINES OT BROTHER RAE,

**A Devoted Freemason, on his leaving for Australia
July, 1885.**

THE sun shines with his brightening rays
    On every land and sea;
A loving brother leaves his home
    To fight with destiny.

May fortune's smiles be wafted o'er
    The ocean's foamy main,
And land our worthy brother safe
    On Australia's lovely plain.

Accompanied by his loving wife,
    No danger need he fear –
His best and truest friend on earth
    His honest heart will cheer.

If landed safe on foreign shore,
    In "God we trust" he may,
To meet his loving boys all well,
    God speed the happy day.

Though many may your friendships be,
    Regardless of your foes,
Have aye a place within your heart
    For the memories of Montrose.

As brothers true, we wish him joy,
    Success for many a day;
An honour to the ancient craft
    Is worthy Brother Rae.

May peace and plenty be your lot,
    Till earthly pleasure's o'er;
When, brethren all, we hope to meet
    On Eden's sunny shore.

MY BONNIE LASS.

I'VE fa'in in love wi' a bonnie lass,
    A smirtsome dame is she;
Her hair is o' the auburn hue,
    An' a twinkle in her e'e.

She's nae ane o' thae pick-me-ups
    Ye'll get where'er ye gang,
But a thoro'-gaen, honest lass,
    An' nae gien up tae slang.

An honour tae her parents dear,
   She lo'es them baith wi' pride;
On Sundays, when they're at the kirk,
   She's aye gaun by their side.

I think I'll pop the question, lads,
   See what she has tae say,
An' if the answer be a "Yes,"
   I'll soon ken what to dae.

We'll gang and tell the minister
   The marriage knot to tie;
An' then what happy days we'll hae,
   My ain wee wife and I.

THE WA'-GAIN' O' SUMMER

THE summer sun is owre the hills,
   Across the western main;
An' mony changes there will be,
   Ere summer comes again.

The cauld winds are soochin' noo,
   Aroun' the gable en's;
The frosty nichts are nippin' sair
   The wee bit ragged weans.

The trees are bleak and withered,
      Their stunted limbs are bare,
Bereft of leaves and foliage,
      Look broken doon wi' care.

Grim winter, wi' his icy beard,
      And fleecy coat o' snaw,
Is chappin' loodly at oor doors,
      His frozen limbs to thaw.

Aroun' a clean an' cosy hearth,
      And cheery glowin' fire,
Where happiness and comfort reign,
      In winter we desire;

So let us strive and do our best,
      While summer breezes blaw;
For sunny youth, like leafy trees,
      Will wither soon awa'.

A RETROSPECT

SOME poets may sing o' the pleasures o' winter,
 Would make folk believe that it brightens the scene;
But hunger and hardship put a' oot o' temper,
 When siller's a' dune, and the girnal is clean.

Let's peep quietly into some homes o' the needy,
 How meekly they bear their sad burden of woe;
While others are niggardly, mean, aye, and greedy,
 Would rob, steal, or herry, from freen' or from foe.

The poor working man, he hangs on at the corner
 To look out for work every day; there he goes –
The picture of pity, sad, sad as a mourner,
 The blae on his cheek, and the drap at his nose.

There's aye a black demon who faces us gravely,
 And looks like a speck on the sheen of our eye;
Shake it off, shake it off, be cautious, and bravely
 Face aye the black spectre, but never say die.

The spring time will come again, frisking fu' cheery,
 The frost, hail, and snaw will be driven awa',
An' the cauld winter nichts, sae lonesome and dreary,
Will soon be forgot, baith in cottage and ha'.

Watch and be ready, for the day it is comin'
　　When a' earthly trouble will vanish awa';
Then, on angel's wings, the true soul will reach home, in
　　That beautiful land which our eyes never saw.

————

THE GARLAND O' MONTROSE

IF spared till summer comes again,
In the good old town some days we'll spen';
A game at golf we'll hae, that's plain –
　　On the bonnie, bonnie Links o' Montrose, O!

Wi' a "Jamie Winton" club and ba',
A "daisy" aff the tee we'll ca',
Ower the bunkers, whins an' a' –
　　On the bonnie, bonnie Links o' Montrose O!

We'll mind upon the glorious days
We've roamed amang the bents and braes,
An' those who joined us in our plays –
　　On the bonnie, bonnie Links o' Montrose, O!

Strollin' alang the glistenin' sands,
We meet auld freends frae ither lands,
We touch oor caps and shake their hands –
　　On the bonnie, bonnie Links o' Montrose, O!

The bearded sire and the beardless loon,
The trig auld maid wi' lanely froon,
The gay, gay lass in stylish goon –
   Lo'e the bonnie, bonnie Links o' Montrose, O!

Mony a winsome lad and lass,
Wha ha'e an 'oor or twa tae pass,
Ha'e a jollification on the grass –
   On the bonnie, bonnie Links of Montrose, O!

Mony a chubby girl and boy
Fa's on mony a curious ploy,
But nane there are them tae annoy –
   On the bonnie, bonnie Links o' Montrose, O!

The little toddlin's, hoo they run
Tae the sandy braes tae ha'e some fun,
An' tumblin' cat-maw on the grun' –
   On the bonnie, bonnic Links o' Montrose, O!

You'd think a flea was at their doup,
As ower an' ower the bares they loup,
Heels ower heid, they get money a coup-
   On the bonnie, bonnie Linnks o' Montrose, O!

We ha'e a garland braid and wide
Aroon' oor toon – the ocean tide –
Aye sparklin' like a comely bride –
   By the bonnie, bonnie Links o' Montrose, O!

To soothe oor achin' heid an' brain,
A plungin' dip in the ocean main,
Then a scamper o'er the lovely plain –
  On the bonnie, bonnie Links o' Montrose, O!

You may roam the country, here an' there,
In search o' health an' bracing air;
But there's nane I ken that can compare
  Wi' the bonnie, bonnie Links o' Montrose, O!

———

KIND WORDS

KIND words, dear friends, will hurt not, nor injure the tongue,
Whoever may speak them, be they old, be they young;
They are worth more than riches or worldly store
To the weary and feeble, a hundred times o'er.

Curb the tongue when angry, think before you speak,
A hasty word may prove a curse and make your friend to weep;
Avoid the use of angry words, put kind ones in their place,
And you will reap a rich reward of honour and of grace.

Harsh words when spoken make the blood to shiver;
Use them not, I beg of thee, or you may rue't for ever;
You may lose a friend thereby, which would vex you very sore,
And tend to hurt the feelings within your bosom's core.

There are times of weariness that come upon us all,
The burden seems so heavy that beneath it we will fall;
A cheery word will raise us up and set our mind at rest,
And calm the dark forebodings enclosed in our breast.

Think on an aged parent bowed down with years,
The voice is weak, the race near run, the eyes are full of tears;
An absent child, returned home, a jewel in their eye,
And when the parents hear the voice, the joy it makes them cry.

Love your neighbour as yourself, assist them if you can;
Have sympathy with all and a kind word for everyone;
Be wary and avoid bad words and those that do them use,
They fill the heart with bitterness and common sense abuse.

When young, our loving parents they taught us how to pray,
To tell the truth and shun a lie and never bad words say;
Alas! Alas! How very few their parents' teaching keep,
And in the pit of vice and crime are oft plunged very deep.

Tears would fill the eyes of men to hear the wail and moan
Of victims in a felon's cell, how they do weep and groan;
Avoid the snares of vice and crime, refrain from these, and try
Duly to make joy sublime your comfort when you die.

————

Kind words are sweet to all;
     The heart they lighten and cheer,
With solace sweet enthral,
     Yea, our very souls revere.

Kind words, O! hide them not,
     But use them freely to all;
You'll ne'er regret, I wot,
     The great good they will install.

Kind words, how sweet they sound;
     Like a ringing cheer, they bring
Relief where sorrow found
     A sharp and poisonous sting.

Kind words hurt not the tongue;
     Believe me friends it is true,
Souls from vice they've wrung –
     'Tis not known the good they do.

Kind words, worth more than gold,
      Or rare pearls in a crown;
They cheer the heart so cold,
      That with grief is broken down.

Kind words are soothing balm
      To the weary and the sick;
Vile passion oft they calm –
      Yes, like magic, done so quick.

Kind words our motto be
      In our sharpened witticism;
And hurt not wilfully
      With our rigid criticism.

———

THE FLO'ER O' LILLIESLEA

On a lovely, bricht spring e'enin',
      When the hawthorn was in bloom,
I wander'd oot by Scotstounhill,
      Frae Glasgow's smoky gloom;
The air was fill'd wi' fragrance
      Frae ilka bush and tree;
There I met Jeannie Ferguson,
      The flo'er o' Lillieslea.

I kindly ask'd her for a walk
  Doon by the banks o' Clyde:
Richt willingly she did consent,
  An' sune was by my side;
I took her in my fond embrace,
  An' the sweet lips did pree
O' bonnie Jeannie Ferguson,
  The flo'er o' Lillieslea.

When partin' at the rustic style,
  Beneath a cloudless sky,
We promised there to meet again
  Some e'enin' bye an' bye.
Noo in my sleep I ofttimes dream
  The smiling face I see
O' winsome Jeannie Ferguson,
  The flo'er o' Lillieslea.

Next Hogmanay I'll marry her,
  Mak' her a happy bride;
We'll mind upon that e'enin' walk,
  Doon by the banks o' Clyde.
I'll cherish her wi' tender care
  Unitl the day I dee:
My bonnie Jeannie Ferguson,
  The flo'er o' Lillieslea.

A TRIBUTE TO THE MEMORY OF ROBBIE BURNS

ALL nature's charms are sweet and kind,
They please the eye and fill the mind,
With pleasure's cup the heart they bind –
  An Robbie kenn'd them a'.

The birdie sang in wood and glen,
The murmuring burnie in the den,
Unseen, unheard by common men –
  But Robbie heard them a'.

The star that shines in azure skies,
The wounded hare that maiméd lies;
The aged and worn that poortith tries –
  Yea, Robbie saw them a'.

The modest gowan wat wi dew,
The moosie scamperin' past his ploo,
His faithfu' doggie, tried and true –
  Aye, Robbie cared for a'.

Loved Mary Campbell's winsome face,
And fair Eliza's angel grace,
His bonnie Jean in fond embrace –
  Kind Robbie lo'ed them a'.

The poets are a social clan –
The essence of immortal man;
Deny it, dare you, if you can –
　　　Wi' Robbie chief o' a'.

He nobly climbed the hill of fame,
And won the muse, the fickle dame
Whose mantle wraps his hallowed name,
　　　An' croons him king o' a'.

His faithful friends o'er all the land
With one accord join hand in hand;
Who does not for his honour stand
　　He's nae o' man ava'.

————

THE HOOSIE ON THE BRAE

On the broo o' a hill i' the Mearns
　　　A grey farm steading stands;
Where the sun spreads bricht i' the mornin'
　　　His mantle o'er the lands.
A bonnie greenwood aroon' it grows,
　　　The rowan an' the slae,
To shelter frae the norlan' blast,
　　　The hoosie on the brae.

When I was a laddie years ago,
    Just breekit an' nae mair,
A' sittin aroon' the cheery fire,
    'Twas cosy to be there.
My mither, bless her, sang, oh, so sweet,
    Sangs lichtsome, ithers wae;
Noo wha cudna lo'e to dwell within
    The hoosie on the brae.

My father wrocht hard frae morn to nicht,
    With willin' heart and hand;
To till an' sow, and to make grass grow,
    And fertilize the land.
That the horse may feed on corn an' hay,
    Cattle on neeps an' strae;
An' grim want ne'er poked his nose into
    The hoosie on the brae.

When bairnies we toddled to the schule,
    Oor books tied in a strap,
Wi' a penny safely in oor pouch,
    To pay oor dinner bap.
And Baubie, wha kept a little shop,
    Aye ken'd what best to hae
That wad please the scholars that cam frae
    The hoosie on the brae.

In the e'enins, when the silv'ry mune
       Shone clear as sunny sky,
We ran roon' the stacks at barley-brax,
       Playin' tig an' high-spy.
When an unca voice sometimes cried "boo,"
       We wondered whar't cam' frae;
Ye may guess we sune were a' inside
       The hoosie on the brae.

The guid neibours roon' the countra side
       Made's welcome to their ha',
And mony a glorious nicht we had,
       Aroon' their ingles a'.
A kind guidnicht, an' a haste-ye-back,
       Was a' they had to say,
Syne steered a coorse to that happy hame –
       The hoosie on the brae.

We're a' awa' frae the hoosie noo,
       Nae mirth nor joy is there;
An' nae smoke comes frae the auld lum heid,
       The wa's are bleak and bare.
The grey owlet screeches his eerie cry,
       The raven croaks his lay,
An' the bat flees roon' wi' silent wings
       The hoosie on the brae.

Yet I lo'e to wander 'mang the braes,
        An' hear the ocean roar;
Which brings to my mind the schoolboy days
        We scampered on the shore.
An' the memories o' bygane years,
        Of schulemates – where are they?
Who were dear lo'ed chums, an' played aroon'
        The hoosie on the brae.

We oft look back on oor youthfu' days,
        An' wish we'd aye been young;
It canna be, we maun journey on,
        Life's in a balance hung.
But I'll rest content as years roll on,
        And wait the final day;
But as long's I live I'll mind upon
        The hoosie on the brae.

WHEEL OF LIFE

THIS life of ours you can compare
    To nothing but a wheel;
From the cradle to the grave
    We roll about and reel.
We jolt about from side to side,
    And up the hill and down;
At times you'll find us on our feet,
    Sometimes upon our crown.

When ushered first into this world,
    Our course at once begun;
The race of life is on the move,
    The wheels of life they run,
Well guarded with unerring hands,
    To train our youthful years,
And boldly face the rocky road
    Against all foes and fears.

When youthful vigour's on your side,
    Don't blow your trumpet high;
Just glide along quite at your ease,
    With keen and searching eye.
The best run wheels at times go wrong,
    'Twill be the same with you;
You'll need a dose of pick-me-up,
    The wheel a lick of glue.

When doctored, on your speed again,
  With hopes and dreams so bright;
Strong manhood's power is at its best,
  Striving 'twixt wrong and right.
Some get shattered at this stage,
  The wheels get out of trim,
The spokes get loose, the nave is cracked,
  And broken is the rim.

But some there are, with careful speed,
  Slip far along life's road,
And bear their burdens manfully,
  Though heavy be their load.
The race is run, the work is done,
  A whispering sound calls "Time;"
The spark of life flies thence away
  To some far distant clime.

Rolling over the path of time,
  Keep measured step and slow,
And shun the ruts and slippy ways,
  As on through life you go.
As sure as fate the end will come –
  No power on earth can save;
The remnants of life's broken wheel
  Will moulder in the grave.

OUR OLD FOLKS

(On reading the lives of "Our Old Folks" in the columns of the Weekly News.)

THE white hair an' the wrinkled broo,
    The tottering gait and shaky hand,
Tell us auld age is on us noo,
    And on the brink of death we stand.

When we look back on bygone years,
    And bring to mind the days of yore,
At times our eyes they fill with tears
    And mind of loved ones gone before.

But happy times when we were young,
    When courtin' days rolled swiftly by,
My lassie to my bosom clung,
    Are memories that will never die.

Together we have jogged through life,
    Amongst our bairns, and happy been;
An honest man, a loving wife;
    We're auld folks noo; we'll rest at e'en.

OOR TAM CAT

A FAV'RITE wi' us a'
    Is oor tam cat,
Sic a beast ye never saw
    As oor tam cat;
A coat o' glossy black
Haps noble pussy's back;
The sharp e'e o' a hawk
    Has oor tam cat.

A tail near half an ell
    Has oor tam cat,
An' at his breist a bell
    Has oor tam cat;
An' whiskers roon' his moo
Like the horns o' a coo,
To fleg sic like as you,
    Has oor tam cat.

An' if you tramp the tail
    O' oor tam cat,
He's at ye tooth an' nail,
    Is oor tam cat.
He girns his birsey jaws,
An' fists ye wi' his claws,
Like lances frae the paws
    O' oor tam cat.

He's done his pairt richt weel,
       Has oor tam cat;
Gard mony a moosie squeal
       Has oor tam cat.
He scares the dogs awa',
An' nabs the rats an' a';
He has nae fear ava,
       Has oor tam cat.

But couthie to his ain
       Is oor tam cat;
If friendship ye wad gain
       O' oor tam cat,
A fang o' toasted cheese,
Some sav'ry fish or grease,
The appetite will please
       O' oor tam cat.

In winter near the fire
       Creeps oor tam cat,
It seems the sole desire
       O' oor tam cat;
He mak's himsel' fu' snug
Juist streekit on the rug,
His forepaw ower his lug,
       Lies oor tam cat.

He's nae sae brisk and bauld
            Noo, oor tam cat,
He's getting' frail an' auld,
            Is oor tam cat;
He's juist like you an' me,
Slip, slipping doon life's tree,
Sune at the fit he'll be,
            Will oor tam cat.

———

THE PEARLY ROBES OF WINTER

REAL sharp and snell the wintry winds
            Blaw surly ower the lea,
Across the bleak and dreary waste,
            And past the leafless tree;
In gusty blasts it scuds along,
            And leaves its track behind,
Whirling the snowflakes in its flight
            Like the chaff before the wind.

The icicles, like crystal spears,
            Hang from the rocky ledge;
The drifted snow in mounds lie deep
            Close by the sheltering hedge;

The trees o'erhead are draped in white
     With tiny sparkling balls,
Far purer than the richest gems,
     And polished marble halls.

The ponds and lakes are frozen o'er,
     The ice is smart and keen,
The curlers at their roaring game
     Enjoy the wintry scene;
The skaters round and round they whirl
     Among the happy throng,
And, hand in hand, with mirthful voice
     Sing snatches of the song.

The air is bracing and serene,
     The sky is clear and bright,
The sparkling starts like diamonds glance,
     The moon sheds forth her light;
The earth is wrapp'd as in a shroud,
     Whiter than wool can grow,
In Nature's robe of spotless white –
     Pure and beautiful snow.

WEE WILL

A NICKUM o' a laddie is oor wee Will,
For antics and capers he ne're can get his fill;
Trampin' on the cat's tail, or puin's mither's goon,
His marrow, I'm sure, is nae in a' the country roon'.

Whene'er his mither turns her back he's pokin' i' the fire –
Chawin' cinders wi' his gab is his heart's desire;
Mou' as black and greasy as a clorty sooty bag,
It's my belief, to tell the truth, I think he'll be a wag.

For ony decent auld wife wears a frowdy mutch,
He's at her like a ragin' lion, and grips her wi' a clutch;
"Nam, nam," he cries, his greedy gab is gapin' open wide,
A beggin' can't the rogue has got, for hame he winna bide.

Thro' the hoose he hobbles on a four-legged stool,
Gee up my boy; canny, my lad; there now, take it cool;
Wi' an auld stockin' for a whip, a garten for a rein,
Proud as any belted knight wi' jockeys in his train.

Creepin' like a parten, mawin' like a cat,
Thro' the hoose on a' his fours scrannin' like a rat;
Before you'd say Jack Robinson, it's true, I do declare,
Shoudin' on the topmost rince o' daddy's arm chair.

Crickey, what a fa' he's got – my heart, oh dearie me,
That loon o' mine, for narrow shaves, his like I ne'er did see;
A day ne'er passes ower his head without a dunt or twa,
It's mair than I can understand how he gets ower them a'.

Kind Providence may guide him yet free and skaithless thro'
The many daring cantrips that youth is prone to do;
Rough and royed laddies, and the tricky anes you ken,
Are aftentimes the cleverest and jolliest of men.

Never daunt the youthfu' heart fu' o' sport and fun,
For if you do you ruin a life before it's well begun;
Cheer them in their guileless sport, a cause you'll ne'er regret,
I never saw an auld head on young shouthers yet.

ROBIN REDBREAST

WEE Robin Redbreast,
       At the window pane,
Asking for charity,
       Weary and alane.

Welcome is his song,
       And his company;
Treat him as no stranger,
       Make him welcome aye.

Crumbs give little Robin
        For his merry song;
It cheers the lanely heart
        The wintry days among.

His breast o' soldier red
        And his coat o' grey
Are scanty covering
        To keep the cold away.

Children, love poor Robin
        Shivering with cold,
Out in the winter blast,
        He who once so bold;

You so snug and cosy,
        Happet weel wi' claes,
Cheeks red and rosy,
        Warming your taes.

WINTER HARDSHIPS

THE soughin' winds o' winter,
      The slushy sleet and snaw,
Sae waesome and sae dreary,
      Oh! gin they were awa.

The many wants and hardships
      Puir mortals must endure,
In frosty days o' winter,
      Are hard to bear, I'm sure.

Labourers and artizans,
      And out-door workers a',
Will hail the time with gladness
      You tak' your creep awa.

Hard is the lot o' many –
      A waesome sicht to see
The wee bit bonnie bairnies
      Upo' their mammy's knee,

Cryin' for a crust o' bread,
      Their cravin' wants to stay,
Nae a bite in a' the house,
      Nor hasna been this day.

Tears upon the mither's cheek,
    Her heart wi' grief is sad,
To see her bairns shivering,
    Sai puir and scanty clad.

In the grate there's scarce a'e blink
    To heat their limbs sae cauld.
Mony a dowie story
    This winter could be tauld.

But brighter days are coming,
    Sae do not dowie be;
The darkest days get e'enin',
    Surmount them all will ye.

POOR AND NEEDY

POOR and needy is a waesome cry,
It melts the hearts of passers by;
Shivering beggars we daily meet,
At our open doors and on the street.

Poor and needy in a Christian land!
Let us open our liberal hand,
And give a mite or a crust of bread,
With showers of blessing on our head.

Poor and needy and benumbed with cold,
In an attic room both frail and old,
Scarce covered from the frost and snow,
Whom grim King Death will soon lay low.

Poor and needy is the drunkard's child,
Reared like a lion in the forest wild;
"None to pity him, none to caress,"
A ruined life through drunkenness.

Poor and needy, despised and spurned,
With aching limbs from the door been
turned,
With feelings and intentions just:
It is hard to bear, but bear they must.

Poor and needy, oh! watch and beware
How easy led to Vanity's snare;
Curb the passion of haughty pride,
And all the evils of life deride.

JOUK AND LET IT GAE BY

WE'RE frettin' an girnin' habitually,
  Tae please nae ane need try;
And annoyed wi' crosses continually,
  Just jouk and let them gae by.

Some chield is upbraidin' oor character,
  In the public ears, oh fie;
Let us button oor coats, and knack oor thumbs,
  And jouk and let it gae by.

Some black surly dog has crossed oor path,
  At oor trousers' leg let fly;
Give a kindly pat or a savoury bone,
  And jouk and let him gae by.

A' oor traps are set for a jaunting day,
  Hoping it will keep dry;
Confound it, the rain in torrents does pour,
  Just jouk and let it gae by.

A cove wi' a cane and a surtou' coat,
  A hat on his head awry,
Walked up to me and asked for my wife,
  I jouked and let him gae by.

There's a charming maid with pouting lips
       I fain on would cast my eye;
But my wife, do you see, there is the rub,
       I'll jouk and let her gae by.

In the newspapers each day, "Invest" you'll see,
       In letters both broad and high;
"To sell my hen in a rainy day." Na,
       I'll jouk and let it gae by.

A packman exposin' his goods to view,
       Rare bargains, and cheap, oh my;
Well, no, there is nothing I actu'lly want,
       I'll jouk and let him gae by.

If involved in debt, and unfit to pay,
       You'd better be sleek and sly;
For the beagles will howk and herry your byke,
       So jouk and let them gae by.

Keep a look out in your actions, my boys,
       And open your weather eye;
So when any black speck appears in view,
       Just jouk and let it gae by.

HOOLIE WI' YER HOADLIN' AWEE

'TIS lichtsome when coortin' a winsome young maid,
    Wi sic daffin' and sportin' an' glee,
An' a quiet hour at e'en, baith rowed in a'e plaid –
    But hoolie wi' yer hoadlin' awee.

An' when ye mairry the lassie o' yer choice,
    Remember the busy, busy bee;
Keep the croon o' the causey, laugh and rejoice –
    But hoolie wi' yer hoadlin awee.

An' when wee toddlin' bairns gather round oor hearth,
    An' their antics and capers we see,
Nae happier moments we meet wi' on earth –
    But hoolie wi' yer hoadlin' awee.

A clean, cosy hame, an' cheery ingle end,
    It's there where true love aye should be;
Where socks are to darn, an' breekies are to mend –
    But hoolie wi' yer hoadlin' awee.

Sometimes a bit racket will get up – do yer best –
    In the quietest o' hames, you'll agree;
Dinna lose yer temper, tak' it as a jest,
    An hoolie wi' yer hoadlin' awee.

The laddies may grow up to be bearded men,
    An' the lassies brave women may be;
But it's best nae to brag, lest they fail i' the en',
    Sae hoolie wi' yer hoadlin' awee.

Let's aye do the best for a' freen's that we ha'e,
    An' oor enemies' fau'ts a' forgie;
We'll easier lie when we slip ower the brae –
    Sae hoolie wi' yer hoadlin awee.

THE BRAES OF ST. CYRUS

A REMINISCENCE OF SCHOOL-BOY DAYS

WEEL dae I min' when a laddie at schule,
        Sae happy and cheery and gay;
In the bright sunny days, when schule was ower,
        To the braes we scampered away.

Nae coont nor care oppress'd our young minds –
        Our hearts were quite buoyant and free –
As we speeled the braes in aerial flight,
        Far aboon the murmuring sea.

Hardy and fearless, nae cowards were we,
        In oor cantrips amang the braes;
Up the rugged face of the craggy "Flake,"
        We scaled with the greatest of ease.

Ilk cranny an' cave – we rummag'd them a';
        Naething worth of note did we pass;
We climbed the poles o' the fishermen's nets,
        And pranked wi' "Sultan," the ass.

When wearied and tired wi' daffin' an' sport,
        To the Auld Kirkyaird we would hie –
The hallow'd spot, 'tween the cliffs and the sea,
        Where Beattie, the poet, doth lie.

When gloamin' appeared we hied awa' hame,
    As oor tasks were a' yet to learn;
For the tawse o' Allan, the dom'nie, we feared;
    Though couthie and kind, he was stern.

Where are my comrades? I've lost near them a';
    I doot they're nae a' to the fore;
Some wan'ert a bit, some laid in their grave,
    Ithers treading a foreign shore.

Where'er they may be, their hearts aye will burn
    Wi' thoughts o' the days that are gane;
When the pleasures o' youth, saie sweet tae a',
    We're indulg'd in by ilka ane.

Thae days are past an' will ne'er come again,
    But their memory ever will shine
I' the bosoms o' those who used to roam
    On the braes o' St Cyrus langsyne.

THE CENSUS

The following conflict occurred between one of the enumerators and
a certain man's wife in a certain district in Montrose. Now, since they
have come to understand each other better, they have granted
permission to the Editor of the Review to print a sketch of their battle
over the census. – April, 1881.

WEEL, John, a chiel, wi' pen and ink,
Ca'd here this day, and, what d'ye think,
He asked yer name, then ga'e a wink,
    An' speired if you'd a' your census.

My blood got warm; it was nae use,
He laughed and ga'e me sair abuse;
Syne wander'd a'gate thro' the hoose,
    An' aye he mentioned the census.

He squatted him down upon a chair,
Then asked if folk lived up the stair,
'The truth I want, and naething mair,'
    Said the chiel wad lost his census.

A paper frae his pooch he drew,
An' questions then he asked nae few;
An', if I didna answer true,
    He'd deprive me o' my census.

How many rooms are in yer hoose?
Come tell me now, ye glaiket goose!
These words gar'd me my temper lose,
Then I showed him my census.

I boldly seized the water pail,
The catched the man by the coat tail;
A shower bath his ire did quail,
An' it brocht him to his census.

He swore he'd tell the Registrar,
Who'd bring me up before the bar,
Says he, "That is the place for war;
An' it's there they'll test yer census."

He threw the paper on the floor,
Then made his exit by the door;
My fit gaed whish, he then did roar,
"O! you've jummel'd a' my census."

THE THISTLE

Brave emblem of our native land,
    So rustic and so bold,
Long may you rear your noble head –
    By Scotland's sons extoll'd.

Your jaggy fangs, like pointed spears,
    Protect your rustic crown;
Always unsheathed, and ready aye
    To hew intruders down.

By Nature nurs'd and watered,
    No cultur'd hand thee tend;
Yet up you shoot your lofty crest,
    Your honour to defend.

In bog, on heath, and mountain brow,
    On cairn, strath, and glen –
There may be seen your burry head,
    A true, yet stern frien'.

Though sharpen'd prongs you circle round,
    To guard against your foes,
Protect old Ireland's shamrock green,
    And England's bonnie rose.

THE BANKS O' THE LUTHER

BY the banks o' the Luther – that wimpling burn
Thro' the Howe o' the Mearns tak's mony a turn –
In the calm evening twilight there did repair
Young Willie, sae brave, and sweet Jessie, sae fair.

Oh, sweet were their greetings as aft as they met;
Happy their partings at the auld garden yett.
Their hearts beat as one though their bodies were twain;
An' Willie lo'ed Jessie, for she was his ain.

Noo their rovings are o'er, and the victory won;
These twa loving hearts noo are joined intae one.
Come weal or come woe, they life's burdens will share,
Young Willie, sae brave, and his Jessie, sae fair.

The bright glow o' true love aye shines in their ha',
And the veil o' contentment 'roun' them does fa';
Aye couthie and kind tae a neibour or friend;
May joy fill their cups, and sweet bliss be their end.

APRIL

RICH are thy blessings,
    Thou gay month of Spring;
Earth in new dressings;
    The birds blithely sing.

Flowers are springing;
    The meadows are green;
Maidens are singing
    While washing at e'en.

The birds build their nests
    In the shady grove,
And the shepherd rests
    Where the lambkins rove.

The ploughman is gay
    As he sows the seed,
For a future day
    Man and beast to feed.

The gloom of Winter
    Now passes away;
Bright shadows glinter
    On an April day.

OOR FIRESIDE AT E'EN

WHEN the toils o' the day are a' at an end,
   The yoke o' oppression seems broken in twa;
And my spirits are licht as homeward I wend,
   To romp wi' the bairnies, and hear their guffa'.

Wee todlins, he runs his da-da fond to meet,
   His snawy-white daidle sae neat an' sae clean;
His airmies extended, wi' joy like tae greet,
   Tae welcome me hame tae oor fireside at e'en.

When supper is over, and dishes set by,
   Roon' the cheery bit fire in a circle we sit,
An' the beam o' contentment moistens each eye,
   While baudrons she purrs on the rug at oor fit.

In my auld armchair a bit smoke I then tak',
   Sends the reek up the lum – for a's clean's a new preen;
And Tibbie an' me hae a social bit crack
   On the news o' the day, at oor fireside at e'en.

The tasks are tae speir, an' when a' answered richt,
   The bairnies some hairmless diversion maun ha'e;
Sae, tae please them, I try thro' the lang forenicht,
   An' join in their mirth an' their innocent play.

Whiles jinkin' roon' the chairs, playin' at the ba',
    Or shootin' little sodgers, like marksmen keen,
Makin' droll figures wi' my hands on the wa' –
    Funny tricks are tried at oor fireside at e'en.

Wi' sic daffin' an' sport the time passes by;
    But their wee eekie peekers begin tae blink;
Syne awa' tae their nest, as warm as a pie,
    An' in each ither's arms fu' closely they link.

They list their wee prayer tae their Maker aboon,
    Tae guard an' protect them frae dangers unseen;
A sweet kiss frae their ma – noo a' sleepin' soon' –
    Sae these are the joys o' oor fireside at e'en.

O' ye wha are bless'd wi' a cosy bit hame,
    A kin' loving wife, an' some rosy-cheek'd weans,
Aye cheerily join in their innocent games,
    An' feel that your heart tae their interest leans.

In yer ain fam'ly circle there you sud be,
    The king o' amusement sae bricht an' sae keen;
That is the place where true joy you will see,
    If the lamp o' love shines at the fireside at e'en.

THE BONNIE WOODS O' CRAIGO.

BY the bonnie woods o' Craigo I love to wander free,
An' down the grassy banks o' Esk meand'ring to the sea,
To hail the cooling breezes beneath the shady trees,
An' listen to the humming of the homeward laden bees.

To hear the linties sweetly sing all in the greenwood shade,
While the sparkling pearly dewdrops adorn ilk leaf and blade;
The glossy blackbird whistles sweet his lovely evenin' sang;
The cushie's coo is heard aloud the bushy firs amang;

While the other feather'd warblers lend forth their merry strain,
An' rich-clad fields are waving with heavy laden grain;
All nature drest in full array, sae gorgeous an' sublime –
A solace to the weary heart an' to the troubled mind.

A fav'rite haunt to lovers true, their faithful vows to tell;
The merry laugh of sportive youth resounds thro' woods an' dell;
Fond parents an' their children roam adown Saint Martin's Den,
To gambol in their childish sports, the e'enin there to spen'.

Thou bonnie woods o' Craigo, to me thou'lt aye be dear;
The happy days I've spent near thee are in my mem'ry clear:
As long's my strength will bear me up, I'll hie me to thy glade,
An' rest my stiff an' aching limbs beneath thy cooling shade.

MARY GARDNER.

A WEE tender flower, sae modest an' fair;
A bright gem of beauty, sae rich and sae rare;
In symmetry fine, for an angel might pass –
Lovely Mary Gardner, that bonnie wee lass.

But hard is her lot in this world below,
For shivering she stands the worst breezes that blow;
On the cold slushy streets the daunders alang
At her father's right hand while he sings a sang.

The rough bustling crowd with amazement they stand;
Sometimes a spare copper drops into her hand,
With a kind loving pat, for seldom they meet
Sic a bonnie wee lass wha wanders the street.

Her mother was laid in her grave months ago;
While she, but a rosebud of four years or so,
Left to roam o'er the country a vagrant life,
And to live 'mid the scenes of cursing and strife.

May He wha looks doon on puir mitherless bairns
Protect her and guard her frae sin's burning airns;
A brand plucked from the fire of folly and crime,
And bathed in the goodness of glory sublime.

A POETICAL EPISTLE
TO "W.F.M'H."

ALL hail! My freen', I'm prood to hear
  Ye blithely sing yer hamely sand,
O' "Luther's" winding stream sae clear,
  An' "Craigo's" lovely "woods" amang.

In days gane by, when ye were young,
  Ye played yersel on 'Cyrus braes;
And noo, I see, their praise you've sung,
  In twa or three bonnie lichtsome lays.

Puir *"Sultan," too, he's not forgot –
  Wha's lugs ye often tried tae pu';
You mind how sweer he was to trot –
  No mony things forgot by you!

But changed and gane are a' thae days
  O' boyish fun an' frolic free;
And noo ye climb Parnassus braes,
  Far, far aboon the like o' me.

I see you noo weel up the hill,
  As I lie scramblin' at the fit;
An' you o' honours get her fill,
  Displaying genius, sense, and wit.

* Donkey.

Frae week tae week i' the Review,
        I houp you'll let your genius shine;
And bring forth things baith auld an' new –
        Things grave, things comic, and sublime.

The muse, tho' fickle, thinks nae shame
        To dwall wi' them o' lowly fare;
And as you've won the saucy dame,
Aye court an' cherish her wi' care.

Lang, lang, my freen', I houp you'll sing
        I' your ain pawky, hamely way,
An' ne'er feel want for onything,
        Nor ken what is a rainy day.

On, on, aye on, your motto be,
        As it has been i' days gane bye;
An' upward aye direct yer e'e,
        Tae Him wha helps a' those wha try.

May joy gang wi' ye thro' this life,
        An' nae grief at your angle sit;
An' when you leave this warld o' strife,
        May you aye on His right hand sit.

A. STEWART

THE BEGGAR'S BAIRN.

ON a frosty night a'e winter time,
Methinks it was in seventy-nine,
In a burgh toon, close by the sea,
In fair Scotland, 'twixt the Tay and Dee;
The night was cold, and the blinding snow
Toss'd the wayward trav'ler to and fro;
The gusty wind with eddying sweeps
Compiled the drifting snow in heaps;
John Frost was keen, and with powerful clasp
He bound the earth in his iron grasp;
The guardians of that burgh toon
Patroll'd their beats, baith up and down,
And scanned with scrutinising eyes
Ilk alley, street, and stair likewise,
In quest of thieves or robbers bold,
And wandering waifs exposed to cold,
And those whom drink had toppled o'er,
When ushered from the ale-house door;
A dark-like object met their gaze,
Among the snow and frosty haze,
With cautious hand they feel with care;
When, hark! a moan, and then a stare
From a haggard face and blood-shot eyes,
Then, lo! at last a baby cries.
A mother, with her child, is found
O'ercome with drink, lying on the ground;

Her child, a boy of three or so,
His ruby lips were all aglow;
On her breast he nestled close and warm,
His home and refuge from all harm.
Though nocht but rags him e'er did hap,
A loving child was the beggar's brat.
The patrol says, and that aright,
She can't lie here this frosty night;
Before the morning light we'd see
She'd cross the shores o' eternity.
With tenty care they raised her up,
But ah, alas! the powerful cup
Had fairly turned her feeble brain;
She tried to walk, but all in vain.
With heavy eyes and stifled breath
She looked as on the brink of death.
An ambulance procured at last,
The drunken wretch thereon was cast,
And rattled through the blinding snow
To the prison-house where drunkards go;
Then locked up in a gloomy cell
To wail and howl her dismal yell.
Her loving babe still hugged her breast –
The pillow where his head should rest.
For drink that night her love was sold;
She neither cared for child nor cold.
With careful hands the child they raised –

Poor thing, he looked like one amazed.
He lisped when severed from her breast
"My mammie – O! I like my mammie best."
A kindly matron washed his face,
Combed down his hair, and brushed his dress,
And warmed him at a glowing fire,
As cosy as he could desire;
A steaming dish of wholesome meat
For supper, then, he quick did eat;
Then laid upon a bed so warm,
Safe from the cold, and every harm;
Nothing left that could be done
To make his lot a pleasant one.
The whole night through ne'er closed an e'e,
But rolled and tossed in agony,
And cried oft, oft, with heaving breast, -
"My mammy – O! I like my mammy best."
Next morning at the break of day,
To the prison-house he wends his way,
Peering forth with his wee, bright eyes
For his mother's form – that wished-for prize.
When, hark! a step on prison stair,
A female form with matted hair
Appears before our gazing eye –
Sad picture of humanity!
Her clothes in tatters round her form,
Her visage grim, her look forlorn,

Her eyelids heavy, dull as lead,
With shame she sadly hung her head.
Her chubby boy, whene'er he saw
That form he lo'ed the best o' a',
With arms outspread in childish glee,
And airy steps so light and free,
He bounded forth, a loving child,
And in her face he kindly smiled,
And cried with joy, as her form caress'd, -
"My mammy – O! I like my mammy best."
O children, love your parents dear,
And cause them ne'er to shed a tear;
Alas! how oft we them despise,
And shun the way which they advise;
Though drunkards, cherish them with care;
If pious, praise them everywhere:
Whate'er they be their affection gain,
For you'll never see their like again!
And whae'er may read, a lesson learn,
Frae that chubby boy, the beggar's bairn.

THE MELVILLE TERRACE GARDENS.

(Dedicated to Dean of Guild Scott, 1881.)

SOME toons may brag o' crescents fine,
Cathedrals grand, and halls divine,
But Montrose it does them a' outshine
Wi' its Melville Terrace Gardens.

In days langsyne when we were boys,
Clad in our suits o' corduroys,
We ne'er dreamt o' the lichtsome joys
I' the Melville Terrace Gardens.

A stagnant waste o' dirty dubs,
Auld fryin' pans, an broken tubs;
But noo a gem o' flowers an' shrubs
Is the Melville Terrace Gardens.

On the bowling green an e'en to spen',
Wi' a faithfu' cronie or a frien',
Is highly prized by working men
In the Melville Terrace Gardens.

O may we a' be spared tae see
The Links laid oot as they shou'd be,
Adorn'd wi' flower, an' shrub, an' tree,
Like the Melville Terrace Gardens.

Montrosians here an' far awa',
If ye can spare a mite ava,
Just send it here, tho' e'er sae sma',
Tae the fund o' the Terrace Gardens.

And when you spend a holiday
Tae view oor toon some summer day,
You'll bless the mite you gave away
Tae improve the Terrace Gardens.

An' he wha framed that lovely spot,
A noble Dean, a true-born Scott,
May beauty aye shine roon' his cot,
Like the Melville Terrace Gardens.

Some narrow-minded, frettin' folk
Wad fain oor worthy Dean provoke,
But a' their chaff will end in smoke –
We'll get a' oor Terrace Gardens.

An' generations yet unborn
Will praise his name baith e'en and morn,
An' pledge his health in John Barleycorn,
For the Melville Terrace Gardens.

Lang may his burly form be seen
At early morn an' dewy e'en,
Out viewing a' the Links sae green,
An' the Melville Terrace Gardens.

For memory's sake, we yet shall see,
Beneath a weeping willow tree,
His statue, by the public free,
In the Melville Terrace Gardens.

A NOVEL CURE.

The ither week, I'm loath tae say,
    A frien' o' mine fell ill –
Puir chiel, he looked fu' sad and wae
    Some sickness fa'n intil.

At times ye'd thocht he was insane,
    Whilst broken down wi' grief;
A' things I tried tae ease the pain,
    Tae give him some relief.

. . . . .

The cures I tried had nae effect
    Upon his case ava;
The doctor says, "I dae expect
    He's wearin' faist awa'."

Laist nicht aboot the gloamin' 'oor
  A knock cam' tae the door;
A lassie, in her breist a flo'er,
  Cam' trippin' 'lang the floor.

An' when she looked upo' the bed
  Whereon my frien' did lie,
O bitter were the tears she shed,
  Heav'd mony a heavy sigh.

With sobbing voice she meekly said,
"Puir Johnnie, where's the pain?
O! Is it in your breast sae braid,
  Or is it in your brain?

O! dinna hanker wi' the truth,
  Come, tell me like a man;
Tae gain again the bloom o' youth
  I'll cure you if I can."

He slowly raised his feeble arm,
  Her hand pressed on his heart;
"'Tis there, dear Annie, O! sae warm –
  A shot frae Cupid's dart.

The doctor fears I'm deein' fast,
  The pain he canna quell;
I doot it's wearin' near the last,
  Fain wad I say farewell."

"O! dinna dee, my Johnnie lad,
     I couldna live mysel';
If I can cure your pain sae bad,
     Juist tak' me tae yersel'."

A beam of joy lit up his face,
     His look was like his ain;
He clasped her in his fond embrace,
     An' lisped, "You've cured the pain."

———

MY AIN AULD MAN

THE wrinkle's on my broo;
     An' my hair is turnin' grey;
I'll soon be at the fit
     O' life's rough an' rugged way.
My bairnies are a' up,
     An' a' married aff my han';
Sae I'll toddle tae life's en',
     Wi' my ain auld man.

My blood is getting' thin,
     Which aye maks me unco caul';
An' totterin' is my gait,
     For I'm noo sae frail an' aul'

I'm prood, believe me, freen's,
>   I've aye done the best I can
For a' my bonnie bairns
>   An' my ain auld man.

'Tis forty years an' mair
>   Sin' in wedlock we were tied;
A lassie in my teens
>   That day I becam' his bride.
The rose was on my cheek,
>   But its' noo grown pale an' wan,
Yet the bloom's aye fresh an' fair
>   Tae my ain auld man.

O lassies, a' tak' tent,
>   When you lea' your faither's ha',
Tae wed wi' the laddie
>   That ye lo'e the best o' a';
Mak' yer hame fu' cosy,
>   An' aye dae the best you can,
An' welcome wi' a smile
>   Aye yer ain guid man.

AULD BETTY JACK.

A DECENT, dainty body was auld Betty Jack,
Sae couthie was her company, an' hamely aye her crack;
A smile aye on her coontenance, though wrinkled was her broo;
A lovin' heart beat in her breast, sae honest an' sae true.

A fav'rite wi' baith auld an' young auld Betty aye had been –
Her marra noo-a-days is rarely tae be seen;
Her sleeves up tae her elbows frae mornin' licht till dark,
Wi' willin' han' auld Betty was eydent aye at wark.

Tae soothe the pillow o' the sick, auld Betty aye was there,
An' gaird her charge wi' tenderness was aye her constant care,
Tho' trauchled late an' early, nae grumblin' dame was she,
Her lot took as her destiny, an' focht it cheerfully.

The little toddlins on the street she'd clap upon the pow,
An' crack a joke tae please the tots was Betty's weel ken'd vow;
She'd lift them in her airms, an' shog them up an' doon –
Mony a smile auld Betty got while others goot a froon.

Tho' totterin' grew her step, and her lyart locks were grey,
Her heart was like the bairnies, sae frolicsome and gay,
Which mak's auld age a pleasure – a lesson tae us a',
Tae be cheery an' contented where'er oor lot befa'.

Her kindly smile, it will be missed at mony an ingle en',
For mony a blithe an lichtsome nicht wi' Betty we did spen';
Tellin' stories about auld langsyne, fu' o' mirth an' fun –
You'd nae believe the nicht was dune, you'd scarce think it begun.

Auld Faither Time he cam' an' took auld Betty in his airm,
An' winged her soul tae a brichter throne tae gaird it safe frae
      hairm,
Which loosed the bonds o' warldly cares, set sin an' sorrow free;
An' we laid her body gently down in Rosehill Cemet'ry.

OUR SILVER WEDDING.

MARY, dear, my own loved wife,
    'Tis five-an'-twenty years to-day
Since hands we joined in wedded life –
    Then you and I were young and gay.

Now we've reached the sunny height –
    Sweet Nature pulled us up the hill,
Through sorrow dark and glory bright,
    Yet aye we live contented still.

Though many have our hardships been,
    We joined aye at each other's call;
Our silver wedding now we've see –
    The Lord be praised for them all.

We've done our best – who can do more –
    And lived as man and wife should do;
The same we'll try life's journey o'er,
    To live and love in friendship too.

For an 'oor or twa their friends all met
    To wish them joy for many a day;
As roon' their cosy fireside sat,
    A happy company, bright and gay.

How sweet the 'oors did steal awa',
　　Wi' stories o' the byegane years –
'Boot courtin' times what did befa'
　　An' hoo they won their lovely dears.

The time slipp'd by, an' friends did part
　　Wi' blessings for the time to come –
A kindly word a loving heart,
　　An long a happy, happy home.

HAUGHTY PRIDE

CONFOUND the pride o' frail mankind,
　　Its sometimes sair to bide,
We see it rampant day by day
　　Ower a' the country wide.

Mankind as brithers should agree,
　　An' spread content aroon',
An' kick the ba' o' base deceit,
　　An' haughty pride knock doon.

Some frail mortals fain would shine,
　　Aboon their brithers a';
But, ah! it only is a sham,
　　Vainglory doon maun fa'.

The sable cloak of righteousness,
     Some men would fain put on;
Saints? No. Creepin' hypocrites!!
     Unknowing and unknown.

The selfish man's a dangerous cad –
     Avoid him if you can –
A wolf wrapp'd in a scarlet coat,
     To hide immortal man.

The haughty pride of would-be men,
     Poor slaves they have to dree
And bow their head, for mercy's sake,
     To vain hypocrisy.

Oh, haughty pride, think shame; oh, fie!
     You're here but for a day;
Cast off the cloak of vanity,
     Ere sunshine pass away.

Let humble hearts content themselves –
     Treat all mankind as men –
For haughty pride and selfishness
     Maun sune come to an en'.

The narrow green, six feet of earth,
     Our mortal bed will be,
Where sinner, saint, and sot shall wait
     Grave immortality.

HEATHER JOCK.

WHA hasna heard o' Heather Jock –
    The Shore Wynd kens him weel;
In fac', the folks aboot Montrose
    Think him a curious chiel'.

He doits aboot frae day tae day –
    For wok he canna thole –
An' spins his yairns upon yon seat
    Near by the Lazy Hole.

'Boot catchin' whales and thornybacks,
    An' crooners, flukes, and skate,
Red codlins, saids, and "conger" eels –
    For nocht can pass his bait.

He used tae sail the salt seas ower,
    Frae here tae Inverness;
But noo he thinks it far eneuch
    The point roon' Scurdyness.

There are some places he frequents
    When drouthy lads are there;
He rins the cutter willingly –
    Jock's sure to get a share.

If nasty corns pain your feet,
      He'll ease you in a crack –
Tae dae the job richt tenderly
      Jock fairly has the knack.

He laughs an' jokes intae your face,
      But does his wark the same;
The corn's awa', the pain's relieved,
      Jock's dune his little game.

Lang may his weel-kent form be seen
      At the Auld Shore an' the Dock,
An' spared tae drink the noble health
      O' her nainsel', Heather Jock.

A FOND ADIEU.

These lines were written as a memento from a young boy to an accomplished Montrose lady, on her leaving for Australia. They were great friends.

Oh, many a happy hour I've spent,
    Loved Mary dear, with you;
But now to foreign lands you're bound –
    Farewell! a fond adieu.

I'll mind upon the happy days
    That you and I have had;
Your kindly smile I'll ne'er forget,
    'Twill always make me glad.

A loving friend to me you've been,
    And joined me in my plays;
My little heart you've fairly won,
    So winning are your ways.

Your graceful form it will be missed,
    At least it will by me;
But don't forget me in your prayers,
    Though far across the sea.

I wish you health and happiness,
    Where'er your home may be;
And peace and plenty be your lot
    Is my only wish for thee.

Loved Mary, once again farewell
    From my little heart is given;
If we ne'er meet again on earth,
    I hope we will in heaven.

THE HEYDAY O' YOUTH

OH happy are the days when youth's on oor side,
We ne'er dream o' care, nor the turn o' the tide;
Sae blythsome and cheery, the time slips awa',
Like a glint o' the sun on the new fa'in snaw.

Rompin' and skippin' a' the road to the schule,
For to be there in time is the golden rule;
With a hip, hip, hurrah, we scamper alang,
Ne'er thing the road weary, nor yet far to gang.

When schule days are o'er, the sad pairtin' will be,
An' leave oor auld hame wi' the tear in oor e'e;
A hamely advice frae oor parents so dear
Will guide and protect us thro' life's journey here.

Ye young lads an' lasses beware o' the day,
For snares and allurements may lead you astray;
Let your comrades in life be sprightly and gay,
But ne'er rude in antics, when larkin' at play.

Be humble and patient, mind what yer aboot,
Ne'er yield to temptation, time will find it oot.
Aye hap yersel' weel frae the snell winter cauld,
It will be for yer ain guid when you turn auld.

When youth's days are o'er, and the journey near done,
With pleasure look back on the time that is gone,
Face boldly the world, and aye tell the truth,
And ne'er let shame fa' on the heyday o' youth.

KATE, MY AUNTIE, O!

THE wished-for day will soon be here,
    Then I'll be free and jaunty, O!
For Jock an' me are gaun to see
    Big Kate, my auldest auntie, O!
      Dirum-e-do-e-do-e-day,
          Dirum-e-do-e-dauntie, O!
      For Jock an' me are gaun to see
         Big Kate my auldest auntie, O!

On Auld Yule nicht we're to be wed,
    Then we'll be snug an' cantie, O!
To snod the hoose an' mak' the bed
    Will Kate, my auldest auntie, O!
Dirum-e-do-e-do-e-day,
         Dirum-e-do-e-dauntie, O!
      To snod the hoose an' mak' the bed
         Will Kate, my auldest auntie, O!

Douce Jock Macgregor, he'll be there,
    And Tammy Hill, so vauntie, O!
An ' Snuffy Cox will say the grace,
    An' dance wi' Kate, my auntie, O!
Dirum-e-do-e-do-e-day,
         Dirum-e-do-e-dauntie, O!
      An Snuffy Cox will say the grace,
         An dance wi' Kate, my auntie, O!

Auld Fiddler Watt, frae ower the burn,
    Where cosy sits his shantie, O!
Will do his best to cheer us a' –
    Especially Kate, my auntie, O!
     Dirum-e-do-e-do-e-day,
        Dirum-e-do-e-dauntie, O!
     Will do his best to cheer us a' –
        Especially Kate, my auntie, O!

The parson, a bit rogue is he,
    At times a wee thing tauntie, O!
I wadna say but what he'd steal
    A kiss frae Kate, my auntie, O!
Dirum-e-do-e-do-e-day,
     Dirum-e-do-e-dauntie, O!
    I wadna say but what he'd steal
       A kiss frae Kate, my auntie, O!

If Snuffy Cox should hear o' that,
    He will kick up a rantie, O!
To stop the parson frae sic tricks,
    He'll mairry Kate, my auntie, O!
Dirum-e-do-e-do-e-day,
     Dirum-e-do-e-dauntie, O!
    To stop the parson frae his tricks,
       He'll mairry Kate, my auntie, O!

THE TRYSTIN' NICHT

THE trystin' nicht is coming, frien's –
　　　Hoo quick the time does roll –
For I'm gaun to meet my laddie
　　　Oot by the aul' Links Toll.

It's in the road by Charleton:
　　　A lovely walk we'll ha'e,
An fondly cuddle on the grass
　　　On yon sweet gowany brae.

We'll whisper a' oor tales o' love,
　　　As couthy as can be,
An' ower an' ower we'll pledge oor vows
　　　O' faith and constancy.

We'll wander on the banks o' Esk
　　　To while the time awa',
Doon by the Knab o' Kinnaber,
　　　Where sea-girt breezes blaw.

'lang the sands to bonnie Montrose
　　　We'll dander, side by side,
Close by that ceaseless melody –
　　　The murmur o' the tide.

Across the green and swarthy Links,
　　With nature's carpet dressed,
My laddie he will clasp me to
　　His noble, manly breast.

An' plant sweet kisses on my lips
　　While in my bosom glow
That secret seal, sweet Nature's gift,
　　Which only lovers know.

At the fit o' the Wallie-green
　　We'll pairt, though rather fain,
To meet, ye ken, at the auld place,
　　On trystin' nicht again.

————

THE AGE OF LIGHT.

In days gane by, when I was young,
　　Folks used to burn the cruisie;
There's naething noo but 'lectric lichts,
　　An' young men getting' boosey.

I'd scorn tae don the ways o' men
　　When I was I' my teens;
But noo a pipe, a pint, a lass,
　　Are young men's bosom freen's.

Tae see them struttin' 'lang the streets,
       Wi' whiffs stuck I' their mou's,
You'd think they were some heroes bold –
       Nocht but a burnin' fuse.

They say this is the age of light;
       If true, I may remark
Night will be here afore we ken:
       Remember night is dark.

Be cautious, and consider well,
       As through life you jog alang;
Aye feel your way with tenty steps,
       Where'er you chance tae gang.

Be civil, courteous, an' respect
       Mankind as brithers a';
Ne'er strut aboon your station, freen's,
       For doon you aye maun fa'.

Content where'er your lot is cast;
       Your neighbours all regard;
Attend your business with a will,
       And you'll have your reward.

LINES ON THE DEATH OF WEE ANNIE DAVIDSON.

Who died at Gatehouse-of-Fleet on 5th September,
1885, Aged 2 years and 8 months.

SHE was a lovely little child,
 A bright and gladsome thing;
And love beat in her little heart –
 A cherub of the spring.

We lov'd her as we lov'd our life,
 And thought we ne'er would part:
But oft Christ takes the little ones
 That's dearest to our heart.

We nursed her with a tender care,
 And every succour tried;
Then we took the last fond look,
 For our lov'd child had died.

We laid her body in the grave,
 Beneath the soft green sod:
Her little soul's now wafted home
 To the bosom of her God.

In that bright and glorious land,
 Where Christ's the shining light:
Wee Annie dwells in safety there,
 An angel, pure and bright.

A LOCK OF ANNIE'S HAIR.

You ask what's this I love so well?
Ah! friends, you know I love to tell;
I'll always cherish it with care –
This curly lock of Annie's hair.

I love to clasp it to my breast,
Where of her little head did rest,
Her voice sometimes I think I hear:
Bur no, she's with her Saviour dear.

This little lock it wav'd with grace
Among the ringlets around her face;
While they are withering in the mould,
To me it shines like burnished gold.

I love to lay it in my hand –
A sparkling gem like glittering sand:
And often to my lips I press
The golden lock with fond caress.

As time rolls on I'll love it more,
And think of those who've gone before,
With mother's tears and cherished care,
I'll guard wee Annie's lock of hair.

THE BEREAVED MOTHER.

An anguished mother moans and sighs
For the loss of her husband and son,
    Both reft and torn from her side;
"It's hard," she says; "but 'Thy will be done.'"

    In a foreign land though cut him down,
Where his body lies in a barren wild,
    Her husband dear; then thou hast
Cut off, alas! her posthumous child.

    Fond mother, weep not, dry your tears,
Rejoice in Him who watches o'er us;
    Be calm and restrain all fears,
For all is safe in the arms of Jesus.

    The trials of life, here below,
Are hard to bear, and ofttimes grieve us:
    The loss of friends near and dear
Are the means to draw us nigh to Jesus.

    His own will is to give and take,
The loved, respected, lost or won;
    Your babe is safe and happy,
So, oh! mother, weep not for your on.

All's for the best; hail, mother dear –
Cast off the gloom on your soul that lie,
Husband and son are waiting
To welcome you to the home on high.

———

LINES TO THE MEMORY OF ANNIE DAVIDSON.

Who died at Newbigging, near Montrose,
7th May, 1874, Aged 22 Years.

FAIR as a flower in rosy June,
A charming, winsome maiden;
Her tender heart aye beat in tune;
With smiles her face was laden.

Beloved by comrades one and all;
Her parents' pride and glory;
Aye ready at the homely call
To listen to their story.

A sister's love, a brither's pride,
The idol of their fancy;
The happy hours spent at her side
Brings back her kindly glance aye.

That lovely star of earth has fled –
    Her maker called her home –
And joined that band, by Jesus led,
    To welcome all who come.

Her loving words nae mair we'll hear,
    Nor gaze upon her features,
Until in glory we appear
    God's loved and chosen creatures.

LINES ON THE DEATH
OF LORD BEACONSFIELD.

The wail of Death is heard o'er the land,
And each heart seems heavy as lead;
With sorrowing minds aghast we stand,
When told – Lord Beaconsfield is dead.

A noble spirit was in his breast,
And sweet hope in his youth beat high –
Up the hill of fame, e'en to the crest,
He would reach it before he'd die.

And reach it he did – yea, proudly sat
On the woolsack fearless of all;
And his voice was heard o'er all the world,
Tho' utter'd in Westminster Hall.

His battle was fought, the victory won
On the morn of an April day;
And Britain lost a dutiful son
When he quietly passed away.

A lesson here young men should learn,
To set their thoughts and hopes aright;
There's a race to run, a name to earn,
To make their life course smooth and bright.

FROLICSOME GAIETY.

A BALLET GIRL'S SONG

I'M fully fledg'd and educate,
    Sweet nineteen years – no more;
One of the smartest girls about
    A young man could adore.

    CHORUS.

        I'm gay on it, I'm gay on it,
        I'm up-to-date, that's me!
           Do ye see?
        I'm a smart tidy elf,
        And I know it well myself,
        But I'm yours if you fancy me;
           Tra, la, la,
        I'm yours if you fancy me.

I'm the pride of my parents' eyes,
    No fault in me they see;
Trained at home with a mothers' care,
    But not tied to her knee.

    CHORUS.

        I'm free to roam where'er I choose,
           By woodland, stream, or sea;
        The shady grove and grass green links
           Are well-known haunts to me.

    CHORUS.

I go the bike in proper style,
    It's nice I do declare;
Oh, my! it's life to spin along
    And breathe the caller air.

    CHORUS.

    Golf is one of my fav'rite games,
      It's manly exercise;
    The ball is hit – a beauty, sure:
      Close to the hole it lies..

    CHORUS.

I'm rather on for rational dress,
    I like the bloomer style,
Compact and neat, both legs and feet,
    No petticoats to soil.

    CHORUS.

To hear me sing it is a treat,
    And on the organ play
Such tunes as "Kiss me quick, my love,"
    And dear "Auld Robin Gray."

    CHORUS.

I'm thorough-bred and sound's a bell,
    An honest pedigree;
I like the lads, but that's nae fau't,
    There's nothing wrong wi' me.

    CHORUS.

If any swain feel so inclined,
 As choose me for a mate,
Please ring the bell at ninety-nine,
 And ask for "Up-to-date."

CHORUS.

———

HOW TO WOO AND WIN

I smile to all the girls I know,
 'Tis courteous so to do;
But there is one, a dear, sweet lass,
 The best of all the crew.

I met her just the other night,
 And asked her for a walk;
"With pleasure, dear," she shyly said –
 How sweetly she can talk.

We strolled along quite at our ease,
 Beneath a starlit sky;
I slipped my arm around her waist,
 And winked the other eye;

Then whispered gently in her ear,
 "Will you be my little wife?"
Right modestly she answered me,
 "I'm yours, dear lad, for life."